SACRED

SATB and organ

OXFORD

T0346712

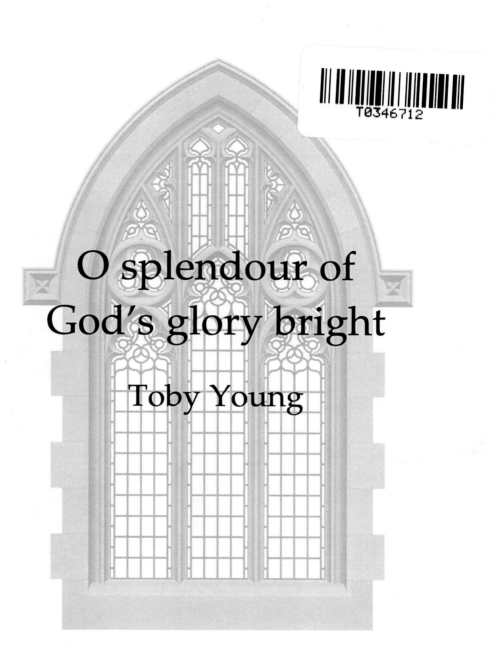

O splendour of God's glory bright

Toby Young

MUSIC DEPARTMENT

OXFORD
UNIVERSITY PRESS

O splendour of God's glory bright

St Ambrose of Milan (*c.* 340–397)
trans. Louis F. Benson

TOBY YOUNG

Duration: 4 mins

Printed in Great Britain

OXFORD UNIVERSITY PRESS, MUSIC DEPARTMENT, GREAT CLARENDON STREET, OXFORD OX2 6DP

4

36

ray___ on___ all we think or do_____ to -

p *cresc.* *mf*
ray on all we think or do.

p *cresc.* *mf*
ray on all,___ on all we___ think or___ do.

p *cresc.* *mf*
ray___ on all we do.

mp 5

41 *mf*
- day.___

mp legiero *legato*
And now to thee our prayers as - cend, O___ Fa - ther

mp legiero *legato*
And now to thee our prayers as - cend, O Fa - ther

mp legiero *legato*
And now to thee our prayers as - cend, O Fa - ther

souls un - sha - dow'd by the_ night.

souls un - sha - dow'd by the_ night.

Reeds (dark)

X827 O splendour of God's glory bright YOUNG

OXFORD
UNIVERSITY PRESS

www.oup.com

ISBN 978-0-19-355906-6

9 780193 559066